LIFE IN THE SPECIAL FORCES

LIFE IN THE
DELTA FORCE

by Chelsea Xie

BrightPoint Press

San Diego, CA

© 2024 BrightPoint Press
an imprint of ReferencePoint Press, Inc.
Printed in the United States

For more information, contact:
BrightPoint Press
PO Box 27779
San Diego, CA 92198
www.BrightPointPress.com

ALL RIGHTS RESERVED.

No part of this work covered by the copyright hereon may be reproduced or used in any form or by any means—graphic, electronic, or mechanical, including photocopying, recording, taping, web distribution, or information storage retrieval systems—without the written permission of the publisher.

LIBRARY OF CONGRESS CATALOGING-IN-PUBLICATION DATA

Names: Xie, Chelsea, author.
Title: Life in the Delta Force / by Chelsea Xie.
Description: San Diego, CA: ReferencePoint Press, Inc., 2024 | Series: Life in the Special
　　Forces | Audience: Grade 7 to 9 | Includes bibliographical references and index.
Identifiers: ISBN 9781678207489 (hardcover) | ISBN 9781678207496 (eBook)
The complete Library of Congress record is available at www.loc.gov.

CONTENTS

AT A GLANCE	4
INTRODUCTION UNDERGROUND PRISON	6
CHAPTER ONE JOINING DELTA FORCE	12
CHAPTER TWO DELTA FORCE EQUIPMENT	24
CHAPTER THREE DELTA FORCE ORGANIZATION	36
CHAPTER FOUR DELTA FORCE MISSIONS	44
Glossary	58
Source Notes	59
For Further Research	60
Index	62
Image Credits	63
About the Author	64

AT A GLANCE

- Delta Force is a special operations force within the US Army. The group fights terrorists, rescues hostages, and protects important people.

- To join Delta Force, people must already be members of the US Army. They must also be at least 21 years old.

- Joining Delta Force requires going through a process called Assessment and Selection. Candidates are challenged physically and mentally.

- After Assessment and Selection, candidates advance to the Operator Training Course (OTC). They practice shooting at targets, making explosives, and gathering information about enemies.

- Delta Force uses vehicles such as Pinzgauers and Light Strike Vehicles (LSVs) to accomplish its missions.

- Powerful weapons help Delta Force perform direct-action raids. Operators use a variety of pistols and rifles on these missions.

- Some Delta Force squadrons specialize in direct-action raids and reconnaissance. Others may pilot aircraft or provide combat support.

- Many Delta Force missions remain top secret. But the organization has played roles in several well-known missions.

INTRODUCTION

UNDERGROUND PRISON

Military helicopters circled over a farmhouse just outside Baghdad, Iraq. Members of the US Army flew in the aircraft. They belonged to a special group known as Delta Force. They had a challenging mission. An American named Roy Hallums had been taken **hostage** by Iraqi gunmen.

Hallums was captured in November 2004. The US military had been working to gather information about his location since then. Ten months later, the military finally had a lead. US soldiers had captured an Iraqi man who told them where Hallums was.

The US Army has been using MH-6 helicopters for transporting its special forces such as Delta Force for decades.

Roy Hallums (center) headed home from Iraq on September 9, 2005, two days after his rescue by Delta Force members.

Dust kicked up as the helicopters landed. Delta Force **operators** stormed into the house. They swept through the building holding loaded guns. They used flashlights as they searched. But the farmhouse was abandoned. The Iraqi gunmen had fled. Hallums was nowhere in sight.

Delta Force operators moved a rug. It had covered a hidden door to a basement. Delta Force members busted through the door. They discovered a small cell. A blindfolded man was in the room. He was tied up. It was Hallums. Members of Delta Force worked quickly to free him. The rescue mission was a success.

ABOUT DELTA FORCE

Delta Force is a special operations force within the US Army. The group was formed in the 1970s for **counterterrorism** missions. The force is organized much like the British Special Air Service. The creator of Delta Force had served with this division. Delta Force is designed to respond to situations quickly and effectively. The force performs many direct-action missions. These short missions usually focus on destroying, damaging, or capturing enemy targets. Some of these high-risk operations involve capturing enemies. Other missions include destroying enemy weapons. Delta Force missions may also involve recovering information.

    Many Delta Force missions are top secret. This means only high-level government or military members can know about them. But some information has been made public. Delta Force continues to work in counterterrorism. Its members fight terrorists. They also rescue hostages and protect important individuals.

US Army members must undergo intense training to serve in Delta Force and other special forces.

To perform these missions, Delta Force members go through intense training. They use special military weapons and vehicles. Delta Force puts its training and resources to use to keep the United States safe.

1

JOINING DELTA FORCE

Delta Force is an elite group. People must meet certain requirements to join this special operations force. They must also undergo training to perform challenging missions.

WHO CAN JOIN DELTA FORCE?

Only people who are part of the US Army can join Delta Force. People must take the

Armed Services Vocational Aptitude Battery (ASVAB) to join the Army. This test assesses a person's skills in a range of subjects including science, math, and mechanics. All Army **recruits** must also complete basic training.

Fort Jackson, South Carolina, is one of four locations where the US Army holds basic training for its recruits. The other locations are in Georgia, Missouri, and Oklahoma.

ASVAB results include a general technical (GT) score. The highest possible GT score is 151. Delta Force members must score at least 110. In addition, people interested in joining Delta Force must be US citizens. They need to be at least 21 years old. People with repeated issues with the law are not allowed to join Delta Force.

Certain skills are required to join Delta Force. Missions may involve diving underwater. Soldiers may have to leap from planes into enemy territory. Delta Force soldiers must be able to scuba dive and parachute. Language skills are useful for missions in different countries. Speaking a foreign language can improve a person's chances of being selected for Delta Force training.

Wearing full gear makes exercises such as push-ups more challenging. For most soldiers, this method adds about 27 pounds (12 kg) to their body weight.

SELECTION AND TRAINING

Before joining Delta Force, soldiers must complete an intense training course. It is known as Assessment and Selection. It includes three phases. The training is

Being able to find one's way with just a map and a compass is an important skill for Delta Force members.

physically and mentally challenging. Just 10 percent of people complete the course.

Assessment and Selection takes place at Camp Dawson in West Virginia and lasts about a month. During the first phase, recruits are tested on physical skills, such as push-ups and sit-ups. They are timed on a 2-mile (3.2-km) run and a 109-yard

(100-m) swim. They must complete these tasks while dressed in full gear.

In the second phase, candidates are tested on their land navigation skills. The soldiers must get to a location using only a map and a compass. They must carry 40 pounds (18 kg) of gear during this selection phase. The soldiers camp at night and are given a new destination in the morning. They may hike 18 miles (29 km) in one day. Candidates must complete this phase with no help from the other soldiers.

The final phase is known as the Long Walk. Candidates must hike 40 miles (64 km) while carrying 45 pounds (20 kg) of gear. Candidates are expected to complete the timed task as quickly as possible. Soldiers who complete the course too slowly will not move forward with

Delta Force. They are not told what the time limit is.

The US Army instructs residents in the area not to help the candidates. George Hand IV is a retired Delta Force operator. He got lost during the Long Walk. He remembers knocking on someone's door and asking for help. The man looked over Hand's maps. He then told him he could take him to where he needed to go. Hand recalls, "He drove fast and left me . . . in the exact same spot I was when I first realized I was lost."[1]

OPERATOR TRAINING

Candidates who advance past Assessment and Selection begin the Operator Training Course (OTC). The OTC lasts for about

Sniper training teaches soldiers more than how to hit targets from great distances. It also teaches them to sneak behind enemy lines without being seen or heard.

6 months. It teaches candidates a variety of skills.

Soldiers practice shooting at targets. As their **marksmanship** skills improve, they begin to fire at targets that are farther away. The soldiers also practice shooting at moving targets.

During the OTC, candidates are trained in explosives. The soldiers learn how to make a bomb using common objects. They are taught how to pick locks on buildings and safes. These skills allow Delta Force operators to enter enemy areas and access information.

The OTC also teaches candidates how to perform surveillance. This means collecting information without being detected. Soldiers also practice using sniper rifles. Additionally, they practice driving skills so they can escape from hostile situations. Delta Force members often use these skills on missions to protect important people, such as government leaders.

Candidates put their new skills to use in drills. They practice in a controlled environment. Candidates may perform drills in buildings, on aircraft, or in other locations. Delta Force members must act fast when situations change quickly. After completing the OTC, candidates officially become Delta Force operators. They are then assigned to a group called a squadron.

The selection process for Delta Force is designed to be challenging. Members of Delta Force are assigned to some of the

DELTA FORCE AND GREEN BERETS

The Green Berets are another special operations force of the US Army. Delta Force's missions are similar to those of Green Berets. For example, both groups perform counterterrorism. But each force is different. Delta Force is much smaller. Green Berets outnumber Delta Force members six to one. Delta Force also spends more time performing direct-action raids than Green Berets do.

The US military likes to keep information about its special forces training a secret. But less information is made public about Delta Force than any other group.

toughest military missions. Most **civilians** do not have the physical and mental strength for these tasks. US Army colonel Jack Jacobs says, "All the kinds of things that scare ordinary people to death. . . .

These are the kinds of things Delta Force loves to do."[2]

The US military is secretive about its training for special forces. But it is even more guarded about how Delta Force members are selected and trained. Dalton Fury is a former Delta Force commander. He shares that these special forces members may have different personalities. For example, some members work best alongside teammates. Others prefer working alone. But he says, "There is a tried and true, very-unique selection and assessment process that is historically very accurate about the type of [person] that will enter Delta's ranks."[3]

2
DELTA FORCE EQUIPMENT

Intense training prepares Delta Force for dangerous missions. Using the best tools for these missions also increases the chances of success. Delta Force operators use many types of vehicles and weapons.

VEHICLES

The Pinzgauer is one type of vehicle operated by Delta Force. It is an all-terrain vehicle. This means it can drive over all types of land. The Pinzgauer can carry up to fourteen people. But only three to four Delta Force members usually ride together. They use the extra space to carry fuel, ammunition, and other gear. Weapons such as machine guns can be mounted on the vehicle for defense.

M2 machine guns and MK19 grenade launchers are among the types of weapons that may be mounted on the Pinzgauer for a combat mission.

LIGHT STRIKE VEHICLE FEATURES

Despite their small size, Light Strike Vehicles offer Delta Force members several benefits.

Delta Force also uses Light Strike Vehicles (LSVs). These are buggies, meaning they have an open top. An LSV can carry one driver and two passengers.

LSVs are designed to be lightweight. Military helicopters and other aircraft can easily carry and drop off these vehicles. Their small size and powerful engines allow the vehicles to travel at fast speeds. They can be driven up to 60 miles per hour (97 kmh).

LSVs can handle rough terrain. Each vehicle has a roll cage that protects the driver and passengers if the vehicle rolls over. Light armor can be added to LSVs for extra protection from attacks. Weapons can also be mounted on these vehicles. They can be attached to the front and rear.

Delta Force members use LSVs for reconnaissance. This means gathering information about enemy forces and territory. Reconnaissance missions help Delta Force and other special forces plan other types of missions, such as raids.

LSVs allow Delta Force members to move quickly in and out of the places where they must perform both types of operations.

Some Delta Force members fly helicopters, such as the MH-6 and the AH-6. The MH-6 is a transport helicopter. It is used primarily for taking Delta Force members to and from their mission locations. It is also used for reconnaissance. The AH-6 is the assault version.

SOAR NIGHT STALKERS

Delta Force may partner with SOAR Night Stalkers. SOAR stands for Special Operations Aviation Regiment. SOAR Night Stalkers fly helicopters such as the Black Hawk. Black Hawks can carry soldiers onto and out of the battlefield. They are also used to deliver supplies. They can even be equipped with powerful missiles and guns.

Weapons such as machine guns can be mounted on this aircraft. It provides air support for combat missions.

WEAPONS

Soldiers in Delta Force are trained to use many types of weapons. The Colt M1911 pistol is one type of gun that Delta Force members may use. This gun was named for the year it was developed. But it has seen improvements over the years. One example was swapping from a steel frame to one made of aluminum. This change made the weapon weigh less.

Hand speaks highly of the M1911. He says, "The Browning M-1911 .45 ACP pistol is a true workhorse of a weapon with Delta."[4] Hand spent 10 years in Delta Force.

He added that in all that time, he never knew of a soldier who chose to carry a different pistol.

The M1911 is easy to load. It can also be fired quickly. As soon as the gun is fired, another bullet is automatically loaded. It will fire as soon as the shooter pulls the trigger again. Guns that work this way are called semiautomatic weapons.

The M1911 can hold up to seven rounds. It can also be equipped with accessories to make the weapon more effective in certain missions. For example, **sights** that project glowing dots can be added to the gun. They make it easier to aim the gun in low light.

Delta Force also uses rifles, including the M4 carbine and the MK18 carbine. Carbines have shorter barrels than most other rifles.

Another useful attachment for the M1911 is a flashlight. This accessory can be used for seeing better or for temporarily blinding enemies.

The M4 carbine is a shorter version of the M16 rifle. The M4's barrel is 14.5 inches (36.8 cm) long. The MK18 carbine's barrel measures 10.3 inches (26.2 cm) long. Defense journalist Stavros Atlamazoglou writes, "This shorter version of the M4 was designed for close-quarters fighting and is extremely reliable."[5]

Although the M4 carbine is shorter than the M16 rifle, the carbine version performs as well as the M16 for targets less than 100 yards (91 m) away.

The M4 can be used to shoot at faraway targets. It has a range of about 1,640 feet (500 m). The gun's stock is collapsible. This makes it easier to use the weapon in tight spaces as well.

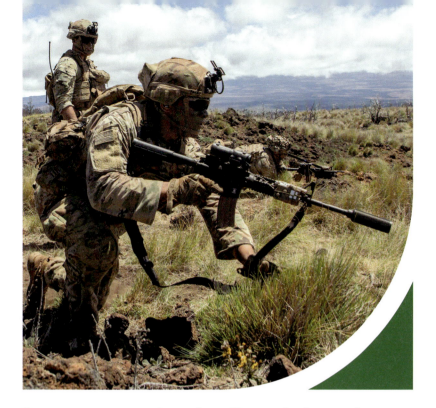

Suppressors are placed on the end of a gun's barrel to reduce both sound and muzzle flash.

Like the M1911, the M4 carbine can be equipped with accessories. This makes the rifle a useful tool in many situations. Members of special operations use a kit called Special Operations Peculiar Modification (SOPMOD). It includes tools such as suppressors and night-vision sights.

Soldiers learning to use M203 grenade launchers use practice rounds for safety purposes.

A suppressor reduces the sound of gunfire. It also reduces muzzle flash, the burst of light that occurs when a gun is fired. The attachment does this by redirecting the gases that exit the weapon when it is fired. Suppressors help Delta Force members use their weapons with less risk of being discovered by an enemy.

Night-vision sights allow a shooter to see the aiming point, even in total darkness.

The SOPMOD kit also includes a grenade launcher that can be attached to the M4 carbine. It is known as the M203. This device can send grenades more than 490 feet (150 m). It can also be used at close range.

The M203 can launch many types of grenades. Some grenades release a bright flash upon explosion. Others release small **projectiles** called buckshot when they explode. Buckshot scatters and punctures nearby objects.

3
DELTA FORCE ORGANIZATION

Colonel Charles Beckwith was an Army officer in the 1960s. After serving in the Vietnam War (1954–1975), he joined an exchange program with the British Special Air Service. There, he led its members on counterterrorism operations in Malaysia.

Beckwith thought the United States needed a similar special force to defend the nation from the threat of global terrorism.

He pushed for the creation of Delta Force. Beckwith said he wanted the Army to have an organization "built upon small

Charles Beckwith is often called the Father of Delta Force. After creating the special force, he became its first leader.

teams which contain mature, professionally trained . . . individuals capable of making on-the-spot judgments."[6]

Today, approximately 2,000 soldiers make up the Delta Force. They are grouped into eight different squadrons. Each has a specialized role.

ASSAULT SQUADRONS

Assault Squadrons make up half of the squadrons in Delta Force. Each squadron can be further divided into three troops. Two troops are used for direct-action raids. These short missions usually focus on destroying, damaging, or capturing enemy targets.

The third troop is trained to do missions without being seen or heard. Members of this troop may include snipers. These highly skilled shooters are trained to hit targets from long distances. Some missions involve snipers killing human targets. But sometimes a sniper's targets are objects instead of people. A sniper can disable enemy equipment with a few well-placed shots. There are also times when these Delta Force members do not fire their weapons at all. In addition to shooting,

PART OF JSOC

Delta Force is overseen by the Joint Special Operations Command (JSOC). JSOC was created in 1980 as a joint command structure for special forces and other units within the US armed forces. JSOC's special forces include the Air Force's pararescue specialists, the Army Rangers, and the Navy's SEAL Team Six.

snipers are also highly skilled at hiding. This allows them to perform reconnaissance on certain missions.

Newcomers to Delta Force often begin their service in an Assault Squadron. Approximately 300 to 400 members are trained to conduct direct-action raids. Delta Force members may then advance to reconnaissance or support squadrons.

OTHER SQUADRONS

Many Delta Force members specialize in areas other than combat. One squadron specializes in flying aircraft. Most vehicles used by the US Army are military green. But some of the aircraft flown by the Delta Force Aviation Squadron are painted in colors of civilian helicopters. This is done

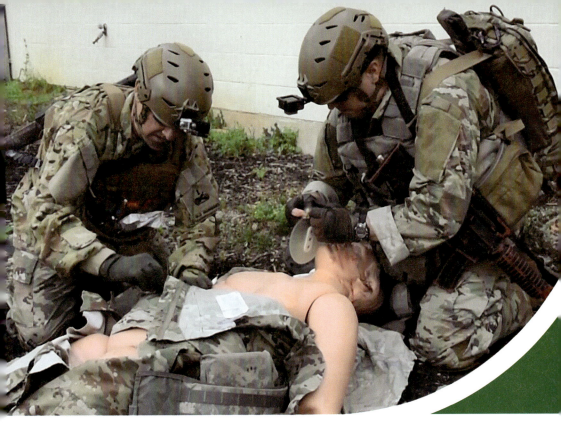

Combat support teams include military doctors. They train to treat injuries that commonly occur on Delta Force missions.

so they don't look like military helicopters. Delta Force members in these aircraft can therefore catch enemies by surprise.

Another Delta Force squadron offers combat support. This squadron includes doctors and weapons experts. Some operators may specialize in disarming

Some Delta Force members train to defend the country against nuclear threats.

explosive devices. Other operators may track and defend against weapons of mass destruction, such as nuclear bombs.

The Nuclear Disposal Squadron's job is to contain nuclear waste. This squadron could be needed if a nuclear facility is attacked. These Delta Force members could also help contain nuclear waste if a weapon is taken from an enemy to prevent it from harming people. Nuclear weapons produce waste that is **radioactive**. If not disposed of properly, this waste can cause health effects such as cancer. Nuclear waste also harms the environment.

Delta Force also has a Clandestine Operations Group. The word *clandestine* means "secret." This group handles some of the most secret military operations.

4

DELTA FORCE MISSIONS

Delta Force is one of the most secretive units of the US military. Journalist Ellen Ioanes states, "The military doesn't officially acknowledge Delta Force. . . . Many of its operations are classified and will likely never be known to the public."[7]

But information about some Delta Force missions has become public knowledge. The special force has been assigned to many types of operations. Its members have rescued hostages and eliminated terrorism threats.

Many Delta Force operations may never become public knowledge. In fact, the US government has never officially acknowledged the existence of this special forces group.

OPERATION ACID GAMBIT

Kurt Muse was a member of the US Central Intelligence Agency (CIA). In 1989, he was captured and held hostage in Panama. Delta Force operators worked alongside other special operations groups to rescue Muse.

A doctor had been treating Muse in Panama. The doctor told Delta Force operators where Muse was being held. He also shared information about the building's layout. This helped Delta Force put together a plan for Muse's rescue. The mission was known as Operation Acid Gambit.

As part of the mission, the US Army attacked a Panamanian government building. This was a distraction. Meanwhile, MH-6 helicopters carried a Delta Force

US Army special forces are trained to land on the roofs of buildings so they can surprise their targets during certain missions.

Assault Squadron to Muse's location. The squadron landed on the roof of the building. The Delta Force members rushed down two flights of stairs to where Muse was being held in a cell. They used an explosive device to break him out. Muse was then given protective gear before the Delta Force squadron brought him up to the rooftop.

IRAN HOSTAGE CRISIS

In 1979, sixty-three Americans were held hostage in Iran. Delta Force members joined other special force units to rescue the hostages. But the US forces were ordered to abandon the mission when disaster struck. Eight US military personnel were killed when two US aircraft crashed into each other. The failure led the United States to rethink the organization of US special forces. As a result, JSOC was created the following year.

Muse and the Delta Force operators boarded the aircraft. But enemies began firing at the helicopters. Several Delta Force members were wounded. But the squadron managed to get Muse to safety.

The whole rescue mission lasted only 6 minutes. General Colin Powell wrote that they were "six minutes that lasted an eternity."[8] Operation Acid Gambit was Delta Force's first successful hostage rescue.

OPERATION RED DAWN

In 2003, the US military helped overthrow Iraqi dictator Saddam Hussein. Policies established during his rule had led to the deaths of more than 200,000 Iraqi people. Many people considered Saddam Hussein a supporter of terrorism. The US military

Saddam Hussein went into hiding shortly after the United States military took control of Baghdad, Iraq's capital city, in April 2003.

removed him from power. But the former Iraqi leader managed to escape capture.

US forces did not know where Saddam Hussein was. The objective of Operation Red Dawn was to find him.

TF 121 was assigned the mission. The task force included Delta Force operators and members of other special operations forces. Approximately 600 people were involved in the mission.

The task force captured and questioned a close friend of Saddam Hussein. He revealed the leader's location. The friend said that Saddam Hussein was staying on a farm. TF 121 found the target there hiding underground. TF 121 captured Saddam Hussein alive. Nobody on the task force was killed or injured. Saddam Hussein was imprisoned and tried for war crimes. He was found guilty and sentenced to death in Baghdad.

OPERATION KAYLA MUELLER

American Kayla Mueller traveled to Turkey in August 2012 to work with organizations providing aid to refugees from Syria. Many people were forced to leave their homes in Syria due to a civil war in the nation. Mueller was taken hostage by the terrorist group Islamic State of Iraq and Syria (ISIS) in 2013 after she crossed the Syrian border to visit a hospital. In February 2015, US officials confirmed Mueller had been killed while in the custody of the group.

In October, Delta Force set out on a mission to kill Abu Bakr al-Baghdadi. As ISIS's founder, he also led it. The US government dedicated the mission to Mueller. It was also named after her. The ISIS leader hadn't been seen alive for

Carl and Marsha Mueller held a photo of their late daughter Kayla at the US State of the Union address in February 2020. President Donald Trump mentioned the family in his speech.

53

several months. But Delta Force began planning the mission when the government learned his location. A couple of weeks later, they carried out the raid that led to his death.

Delta Force members arrived by helicopter at night. When they found al-Baghdadi, he tried to flee. But the special force members cornered him in a tunnel. The ISIS leader knew he had nowhere else to run. He set off the suicide vest he was wearing, killing himself and three others. No US service members were harmed in the mission.

US defense secretary Mark Esper said, "All the praise goes to our service members and our intelligence professionals and others who took this on. And the message is, if you're a leader in ISIS, if you're a leader

Delta Force members have received some of the United States military's top medals for valor. But because the special forces group is among the most secretive, few Americans know the recipients' names.

in a terrorist group we are going to come after you and we will hunt you relentlessly."[9]

Training for the US military is no easy task. But members who show they can handle the most difficult situations may one day join special forces such as Delta Force.

Since its creation, Delta Force has shown itself to be a capable counterterrorism group. The process for joining Delta Force is intense. Only highly trained individuals can accomplish the missions the force is assigned. They use their skill sets along with powerful weapons and vehicles to succeed in dangerous operations. Little information is available on this secretive unit. But the stories that have been made public show that Delta Force has been involved in important missions around the globe.

GLOSSARY

civilians
people who are not members of the military

counterterrorism
military activities aimed at preventing or stopping terrorism

hostage
a person held against his or her will by another person, often to be exchanged for something

marksmanship
skill in shooting

operators
special forces members who have successfully completed training

projectiles
objects propelled through the air as weapons

radioactive
relating to the release of a harmful form of energy

recruits
people who have recently enlisted in the armed forces

sights
attachments to a firearm that help shooters aim

SOURCE NOTES

CHAPTER ONE: JOINING DELTA FORCE

1. Quoted in Stavros Atlamazoglou, "How the Army Used the West Virginia Wilderness to Find Out Who Has What It Takes to Join Delta Force," *Business Insider*, April 13, 2021. www.businessinsider.com.

2. Quoted in Kanutster, "Delta Force / 1st SFOD-D / CAG—'Best of the Best,'" *YouTube*, 2020. www.youtube.com.

3. Quoted in Jack Murphy, "Interview with Former Delta Commander, Dalton Fury," *SOFREP*, February 12, 2012. https://sofrep.com.

CHAPTER TWO: DELTA FORCE EQUIPMENT

4. George E. Hand IV, "1911: A Delta Force Workhorse," *SOFREP*, April 5, 2021. https://sofrep.com.

5. Stavros Atlamazoglou, "Here Are the Weapons and Gear That the US Military's Top Special Operators Never Leave Home Without," *Business Insider*, October 14, 2020. www.businessinsider.com.

CHAPTER THREE: DELTA FORCE ORGANIZATION

6. Quoted in WarIsBoring, "The US Army's Delta Force," *National Interest*, April 30, 2019. https://nationalinterest.org.

CHAPTER FOUR: DELTA FORCE MISSIONS

7. Ellen Ioanes, "Here's What We Know About Delta Force," *Business Insider*, October 28, 2019. www.businessinsider.com.

8. Quoted in Stavros Atlamazoglou, "33 Years Ago, the US Army's Delta Force Pulled Off Its First Successful Hostage Rescue Mission," *Business Insider*, December 31, 2022. www.businessinsider.com.

9. Quoted in Adia Robinson, "Defense Secretary Offers More Details on Military Raid in Syria," *ABC News*, October 27, 2019. https://abcnews.go.com.

FOR FURTHER RESEARCH

BOOKS

Sue Bradford Edwards, *Life as an Army Ranger*. San Diego, CA: BrightPoint Press, 2024.

John Hamilton, *United States Army*. Minneapolis, MN: Abdo Publishing, 2021.

Howard Phillips, *Inside Delta Force*. New York: PowerKids Press, 2022.

INTERNET SOURCES

Robert Burns and Lolita C. Baldor, "Pentagon Releases New Details on Al-Baghdadi Raid," *PBS News Hour*, October 30, 2019. www.pbs.org.

Stew Smith, "Delta Force: Missions and History," *Military.com*, 2023. www.military.com.

"What It Takes to Join Delta Force," *SOAA*, June 8, 2021. https://soaa.org.

WEBSITES

US Army
www.army.mil

The US Army website includes news articles and photos of the army. It also includes information about the army's mission and how it is organized.

US Army Aviation
www.army.mil/aviation

The US Army Aviation website offers information about this branch's history and aviators. Delta Force members who are tasked with flying aircraft are part of this group.

US Army Junior ROTC
www.usarmyjrotc.com

The US Army Junior ROTC website features information about the Junior Reserve Officer Training Corps. This program promotes good citizenship and character.

INDEX

Armed Services Vocational Aptitude Battery, 12–14
Assault Squadrons, 40, 46–48
Aviation Squadron, 40

Beckwith, Charles, 9–10, 36–38
British Special Air Service, 9–10, 36

Clandestine Operations Group, 43
Combat Support Squadrons, 41–43

diving, 14

equipment, 24–35
Esper, Mark, 54–55
explosives training, 20, 41–42

foreign languages, 14
Fury, Dalton, 23

Green Berets, 21

Hallums, Roy, 6–8, 9
Hand, George, IV, 18, 29–30
hostage rescues, 45, 46, 48, 49, 53

Iran hostage crisis, 48
Islamic State of Iraq and Syria, 53, 54–55

Jacobs, Jack, 22–23
Joint Special Operations Command, 39, 48

marksmanship, 19
missions, 6–9, 10, 11, 12, 14, 20, 21–22, 24, 27, 28, 29, 30, 38, 39, 40, 44–57
Mueller, Kayla, 52
Muse, Kurt, 46–49

navigational skills, 17
night-vision sights, 33
Nuclear Disposal Squadron, 42–43

Operation Acid Gambit, 46–49
Operation Red Dawn, 49–51

parachuting, 14
physical fitness, 15–18, 22
Powell, Colin, 49

reconnaissance, 27, 28, 40

Saddam Hussein, 49–51
selection process, 15, 16, 17, 18, 21–22, 23
snipers, 20, 38–40
SOAR Night Stalkers, 28
suppressors, 33–34

training, 15–23, 24, 29, 37–38, 39, 40, 57

vehicles, 24–29
Vietnam War, 36

weapons, 29–35
weapons experts, 41

62

IMAGE CREDITS

Cover: © Getmilitaryphotos/Shutterstock Images
5: © Spc. Sara Wakai/US Army/DVIDS
7: © US Army/SOF AT&L/DVIDS
8: © Sgt. Jason Mikeworth/DVIDS
11: © Staff Sgt. Russell Klika/US Army/DVIDS
13: © Robin Hicks/US Army/DVIDS
15: © Spc. Jorge Reyes Mariano/US Army Reserve/DVIDS
16: © Spc. James Whitaker/US Army/DVIDS
19: © Sgt. Mike MacLeod/DVIDS
22: © Rey Ramon/US Army/DVIDS
25: © Barry Blackburn/Shutterstock Images
26: © Cpl. John Robbart III/US Marine Corps/DVIDS
31: © Cpl. Israel Chincio/US Marine Corps/DVIDS
32: © Davide Dalla Massara/US Army/DVIDS
33: © Staff Sgt. Alan Brutus/US Army/DVIDS
34: © Visual Information Specialist Markus Rauchenberger/US Army/DVIDS
37: © AP Images
41: © Rebecca Westfall/US Army/DVIDS
42: © Petty Officer 2nd Class Henry G. Dunphy/US Coast Guard/DVIDS
45: © Getmilitaryphotos/Shutterstock Images
47: © Spc. Peter Seidler/US Army/DVIDS
50: © World History Archive/Alamy
53: © Kevin Dietsch/UPI/Alamy Live News/Alamy
55: © HQ Vectors Premium Studio/Shutterstock Images
56: © Robin Hicks/US Army/DVIDS

ABOUT THE AUTHOR

Chelsea Xie is a writer who lives in San Diego, California. She enjoys reading poetry and spending time outdoors.